To parents and teachers

We hope you and the children will enjoy reading this story in either English or Spanish. The story is simple, but not simplified so the language of the Spanish and the English is quite natural but there is lots of repetition.

At the back of the book is a small picture dictionary with the key words and how to pronounce them. There is also a simple pronunciation guide to the whole story on the last page.

Here are a few suggestions on using the book:

• Read the story aloud in English first, to get to know it. Treat it like any other picture book: look at the pictures, talk about the story and the characters and so on.

• Then look at the picture dictionary and say the Spanish names for the key words. Ask the children to repeat them. Concentrate on speaking the words out loud, rather than reading them.

• Go back and read the story again, this time in English and Spanish. Don't worry if your pronunciation isn't quite correct. Just have fun trying it out. Check the guide at the back of the book, if necessary, but you'll soon pick up how to say the Spanish words.

• When you think you and the children are ready, you can try reading the story in Spanish only. Ask the children to say it with you. Only ask them to read it if they are keen to try. The spelling could be confusing and put them off.

• Above all encourage the children to have a go and give lots of praise. Little children are usually quite unselfconscious and this is excellent for building up confidence in a foreign language.

Published by b small publishing
This new edition published in 2018
www.bsmall.co.uk
© b small publishing, 1998, 2018
1 2 3 4 5
All rights reserved. No part of this publication may be reproduced, stored in a retrieval system, or transmitted, in any form or by any means (including electronic, mechanical, photocopying, recording, or otherwise) without prior written permission from the publisher.
Design: Lone Morton and Louise Millar
Editorial: Catherine Bruzzone and Susan Martineau
Production: Madeleine Ehm
Printed in China by WKT Co Ltd
ISBN-13: 978-1-911509-63-9
British Library Cataloguing in Publication Data. A catalogue record for this book is available from the British Library.

Get dressed, Robbie

Vístete, Robertito

Lone Morton

Pictures by Anna C. Leplar
Spanish by Rosa Martín

b small publishing
www.bsmall.co.uk

Every morning, Robbie's mom lays out clothes for him to get dressed.

Todas las mañanas, la mamá de Robertito le prepara la ropa para que se vista.

But some mornings Robbie likes to choose his own clothes.

Pero algunas mañanas Robertito prefiere elegir su ropa él solo.

Sometimes Robbie puts on clothes that are too big,

A veces Robertito se pone ropa que es demasiado grande,

sometimes clothes that are too small.

a veces ropa que es demasiado pequeña.

Sometimes Robbie puts on winter clothes,

A veces Robertito se pone ropa de invierno,

sometimes summer clothes.

a veces ropa de verano.

And sometimes he puts on clothes
from his dressing-up box!

¡Y a veces se pone ropa de su baúl
de disfraces!

But today, Robbie puts on his green, spotty T-shirt,

Pero hoy, Robertito se pone su camiseta verde de lunares,

his patterned shorts,

sus pantalones cortos estampados,

one orange sock,
un calcetín naranja,

one striped sock,
un calcetín de rayas,

one blue plastic sandal,
una sandalia azul, de plástico,

one crocodile slipper,
una zapatilla en forma de cocodrilo,

his pink baseball cap,
su gorra de béisbol rosa,

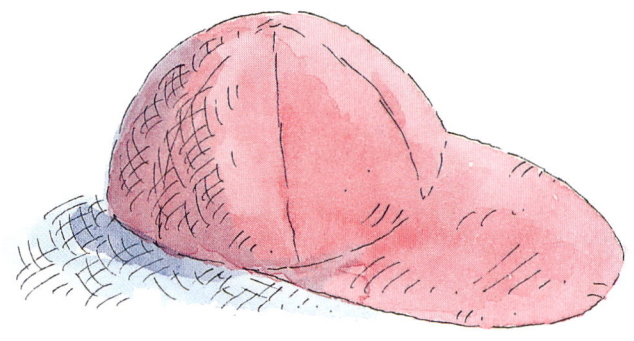

a very long, checked scarf,
una bufanda de cuadros muy larga,

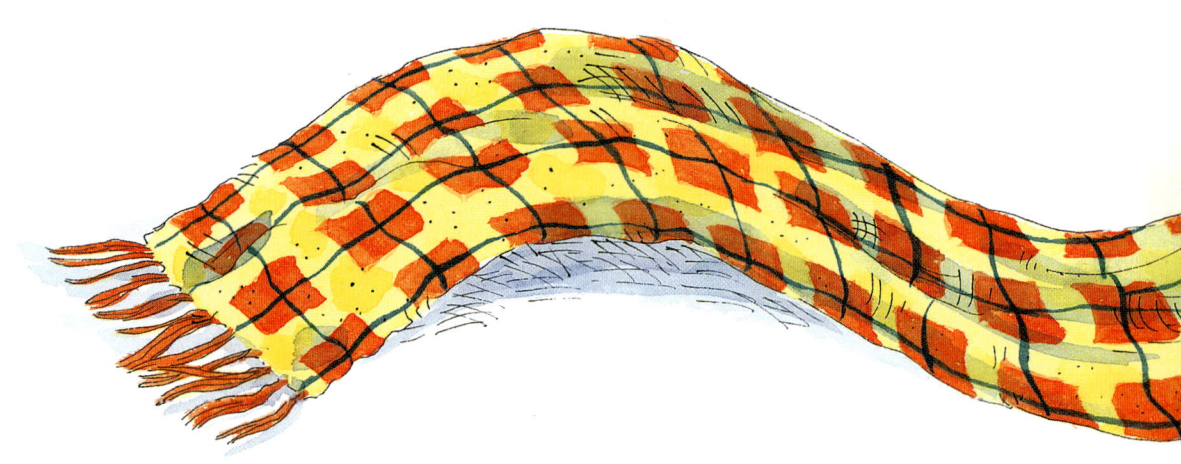

a pair of sunglasses,
unas gafas de sol,

a necklace of wooden beads,
un collar de bolitas de madera,

and his brand-new rucksack with his favorite car and ten coloured crayons.

y su mochila nueva con su coche favorito y diez lápices de colores.

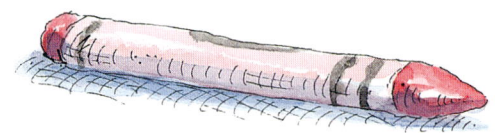

"Robbie, we've got to go out!"
calls Mom. "Are you dressed yet?"

"¡Robertito, tenemos que irnos!"
llama mamá. "¿Ya estás vestido?"

"Yes," said Robbie, "I am dressed.

I'm going to wear this…!"

"Sí", dice Robertito. "Ya estoy vestido.

¡Voy a llevar esto…!"

Pronouncing Spanish

Don't worry if your pronunciation isn't quite correct. The important thing is to be willing to try. The pronunciation guide here is based on the Spanish accent used in Spain. Although it cannot be completely accurate, it certainly will be a great help:

• Read the guide as naturally as possible, as if it were English.

• Put stress on the letters in *italics,* e.g. *roh*-pah.

If you can, ask a Spanish-speaking person to help and move on as soon as possible to speaking the words without the guide.

Note: Spanish adjectives usually have two forms, one for masculine and one for feminine nouns. They often look very similar but are pronounced slightly differently, e.g. **pequeña** and **pequeño** (see below).

Words Las palabras

lass pal-*abrass*

clothes
la ropa

lah *roh*-pah

T-shirt
la camiseta

lah kahmee-*seh*-tah

big
grande

grahn-deh

small
pequeño/pequeña

peh-*ken*-yoh/peh-*ken*-yah

shorts
los pantalones cortos
loss pantah-*loh*-ness *kor*-toss

backpack
la mochila
lah moch*ee*-lah

sandals
las sandalias
lass san*dal*-eeass

scarf
la bufanda
lah boo*fan*-dah

slipper
la zapatilla
lah thapa*tee*-ya

sunglasses
las gafas de sol
lass *gah*-fass deh sol

socks
los calcetines
lohs kahl-theh-*tee*-nehs

car
el coche
el *koh*-cheh

green
verde

vair-deh

orange
naranja

naran-*hah*

blue
azul

ah-*thool*

pink
rosa

roh-sah

crayons
los lápices de colores

loss *lah*-peethess deh koh-*loh*-ress

necklace
el collar

el koh-*yahr*

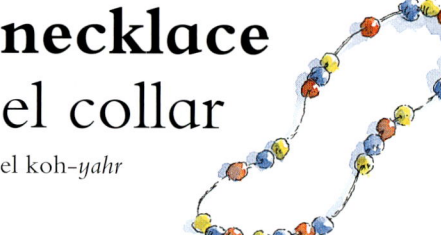

cap
la gorra

lah *gor*-rah

winter
el invierno

el eenbee-*yair*-noh

summer
el verano

el bair-*ah*-noh

striped
de rayas

deh *rah*-yass

spotty
de lunares

deh loonar-ess

checked
de cuadros

deh *kwah*-dross

patterned
estampado/a

esstam*pah*-doh/dah

A simple guide to pronouncing this Spanish story

Vístete, Robertito
*vee*stet-teh, rober*tee*-toh

Todas las mañanas, la mamá de Robertito
*to*dass lass man-*yah*-nass, lah mam*ma* deh rober*tee*-toh

le prepara la ropa
leh preh-*pah*-rah lah *roh*-pah

para que se vista.
*pa*rah keh seh *vee*stah

Pero algunas mañanas Robertito prefiere elegir su ropa él solo.
pair-roh al*goo*-nass man-*yah*-nass rober*tee*-toh pref-ee-*air*-eh eleh-*heer* soo *roh*-pah el *soh*-loh

A veces Robertito se pone ropa que es demasiado grande,
ah *veh*-thees rober*tee*-toh seh *poh*-neh *roh*-pah keh ess demass-*yah*-doh *gran*-deh

a veces ropa que es demasiado pequeña.
ah *veh*-thess *roh*-pah keh ess demass-*yah*-doh peh-*ken*-yah

A veces Robertito se pone ropa de invierno,
ah *veh*-thess rober*tee*-toh seh *poh*-neh *roh*-pah deh ennbee-*yair*-noh

a veces ropa de verano.
ah *veh*-thess *roh*-pah deh bair-*ah*-noh

¡Y a veces se pone ropa de su baúl de disfraces!
ee ah *veh*-thess seh *poh*-neh *roh*-pah deh soo bah-*ool* deh dees-*fras*-sess

Pero hoy, Robertito se pone su camiseta verde de lunares,
pair-roh oy rober*tee*-toh seh *poh*-neh soo kah-mee-*seh*-tah *bair*-deh deh loonar-ess

sus pantalones cortos estampados,
soos pantah-*loh*-ness *kor*-toss esstam*pah*-doss

un calcetín naranja,
oon kahl-theh-*teen* naran-*hah*

un calcetín de rayas,
oon kahl-theh-*teen* deh *rah*-yass

una sandalia azul, de plástico,
*oo*nah san*dal*-eeah ah-*thool*, deh *plas*teekoh

una zapatilla en forma de cocodrilo,
*oo*nah thapa*tee*-ya en *for*mah deh koko-*dree*-loh

su gorra de béisbol rosa,
soo *gor*-rah deh baseball *roh*-sah

una bufanda de cuadros muy larga,
*oo*nah boo-*fan*-dah deh *kwa*-dross mwee *lahr*-gah

unas gafas de sol,
*oo*nass *gah*-fass deh sol

un collar de bolitas de madera,
oon koh-*yahr* deh bol-*eet*-ass deh ma*deh*-rah

y su mochila nueva, con su coche favorito y diez lápices de colores.
ee soo moch*ee*-lah noo*eh*-vah kon soo *koh*-cheh favor-*ee*-toh ee dee-*eth* lapeethess deh koh-*loh*-ress

"¡Robertito, tenemos que irnos!" llama mamá. "¿Ya estás vestido?"
rober*tee*-toh, ten*em*-oss keh *eer*-noss *yah*-mah mam*ma*, ya ess-*tass* bes-*tee*-doh

"Si", dice, Robertito.—Ya estoy vestido. ¡Voy a llevar esto…!"
see, *dee*-theh rober*tee*-toh, ya ess-*toy* bes-*tee*-doh, boy ah yeh-*var* ess-toh